TROPICAL RAINFOREST

GLOUCESTER PRESS
New York·London·Toronto·Sydney

© Aladdin Books 1991

First published in
the United States in 1991 by
Gloucester Press
387 Park Avenue South
New York, NY 10016

Design: David West
Children's
Book Design
Editor: Fiona Robertson
Illustrator: James Macdonald

Library of Congress
Cataloging-in-Publication Data

Bright, Michael.
Tropical rainforest / Michael
Bright.
p.   cm. -- (World about us)
Includes index.
Summary: Explains what
rainforests are and why they are
important, how they are being
destroyed, the effects of such
deforestation on the
environment, and what is being
done to halt the destruction.
ISBN 0-531-17301-1
1. Rainforest ecology--Juvenile
literature. [1. Rainforests. 2.
Rainforest ecology. 3. Ecology.]
I. Title. II. Series: Bright,
Michael, World about us.
QH541.5.R27B75   1991
333.75'0913--dc20
90-44680   CIP   AC

Printed in Belgium

Contents

Introduction

A tropical rainforest is a very special place. It is alive with the greatest number of plants and animals found anywhere on earth. In this noisy, colorful place, forest people have lived together with plants and animals for millions of years. But every second of every day a piece of rainforest the size of a football field is now being destroyed. A precious store of plants and animals is disappearing, perhaps for ever.

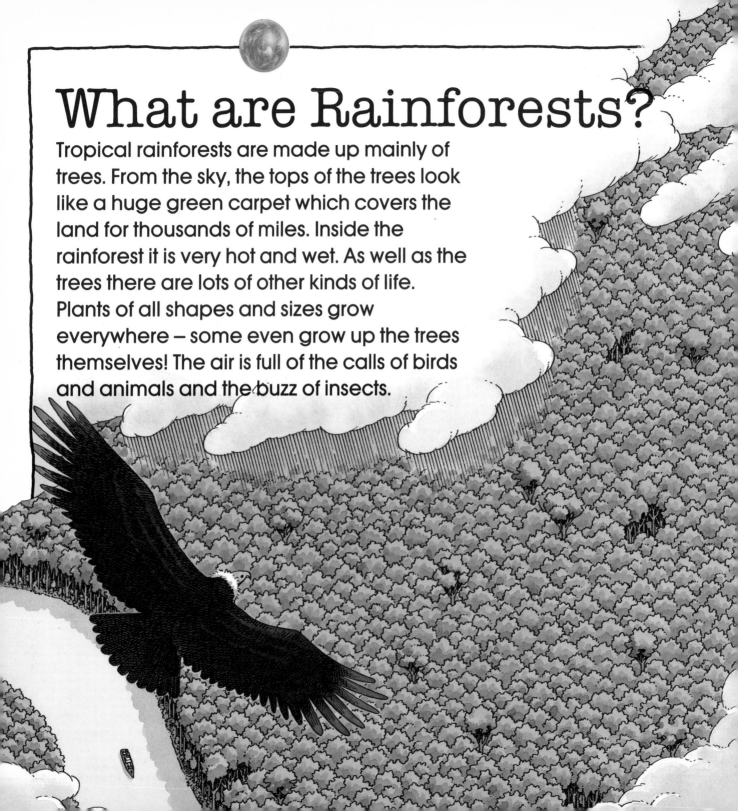

What are Rainforests?

Tropical rainforests are made up mainly of trees. From the sky, the tops of the trees look like a huge green carpet which covers the land for thousands of miles. Inside the rainforest it is very hot and wet. As well as the trees there are lots of other kinds of life. Plants of all shapes and sizes grow everywhere – some even grow up the trees themselves! The air is full of the calls of birds and animals and the buzz of insects.

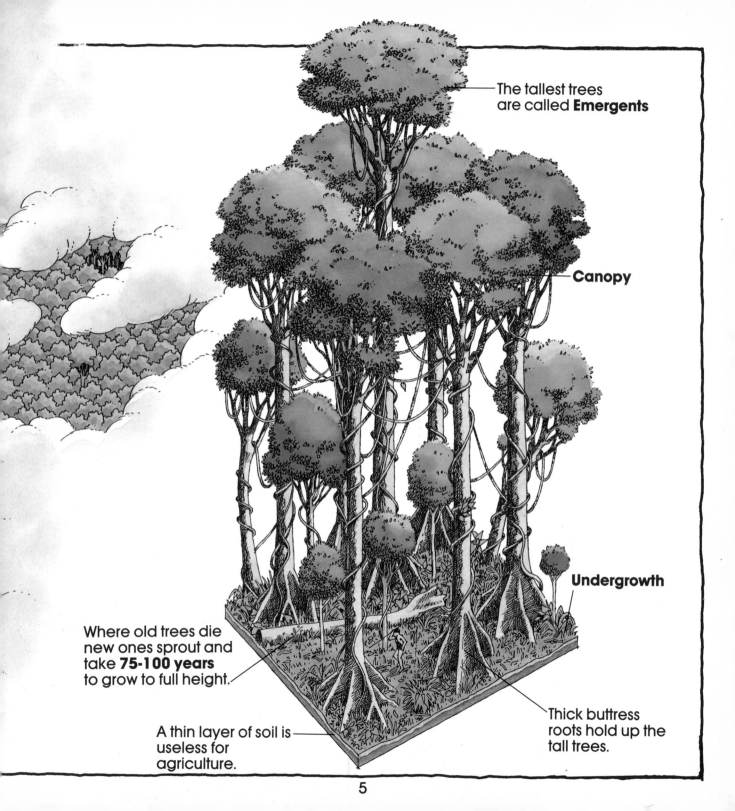

The tallest trees are called **Emergents**

Canopy

Undergrowth

Where old trees die new ones sprout and take **75-100 years** to grow to full height.

Thick buttress roots hold up the tall trees.

A thin layer of soil is useless for agriculture.

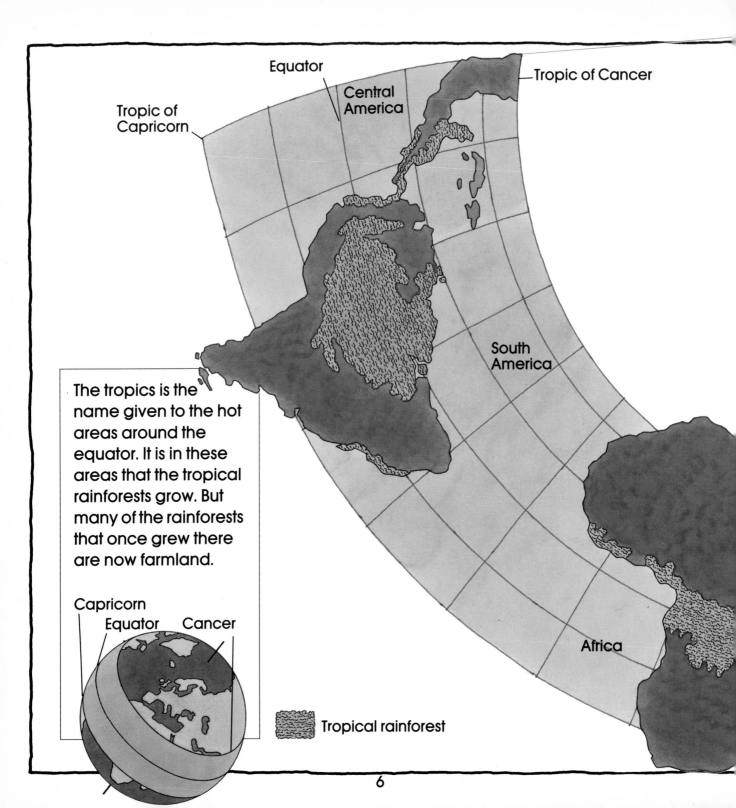

Equator

Central America

Tropic of Cancer

Tropic of Capricorn

South America

The tropics is the name given to the hot areas around the equator. It is in these areas that the tropical rainforests grow. But many of the rainforests that once grew there are now farmland.

Capricorn

Equator Cancer

Africa

Tropical rainforest

Where are they?

Tropical rainforests are found on all the continents that lie near the equator. This is the imaginary line we draw around the middle of the earth. The forests grow in the places where it is always hot and wet. Today the largest rainforest can be found around the Amazon River in South America although huge areas have recently been destroyed.

The map shows where the world's tropical rainforests are found.

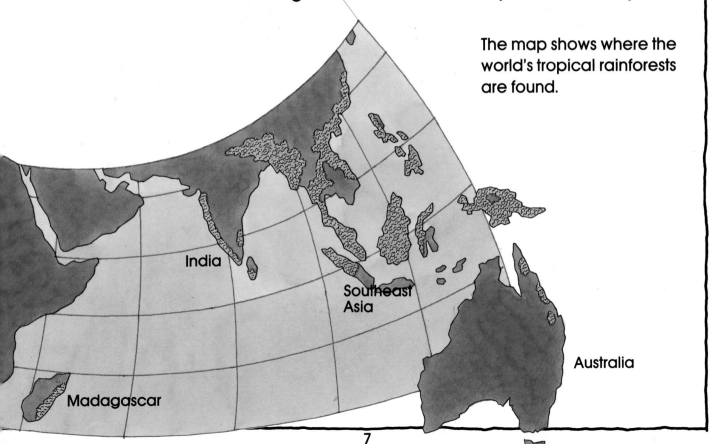

India

Southeast Asia

Australia

Madagascar

In the canopy

A tropical rainforest has lots of different layers. At the top there are a few very tall trees, called emergents. Below the emergents there is a leafy roof, called the "canopy." The canopy acts like a kind of umbrella. It gets most of the sunlight and the rainfall. Brightly colored birds, like toucans and macaws, live in the canopy, as do small mammals, like squirrel monkeys.

Many of the birds have specially shaped beaks to help them find food like fruit and nuts. Monkeys have long tails to keep them from falling as they leap from tree to tree.

Toucan

Macaws

Thorn shield bug

Tree snake

Praying mantis

Squirrel
monkeys

Howlers

Allens opossum

Sloth

Understory

The part of the forest under the canopy is called the understory. The understory is a place of shade. Trees also grow here, but are much smaller than the ones that grow in the canopy. Large animals, like gorillas and leopards, live in the understory. Many of these animals have special markings to match the color of the bushes. This is called camouflage and is one way animals can hide from their enemies.

Chimpanzee

Decomposition
Rainforest soils are not rich. Leaves on the forest floor rot and turn into "food" which is soon used up by the trees.

Fungi eat into fallen branches and twigs.

Insects crunch up dead plant material.

Bacteria in the soil break down everything that remains.

Leopard

Four striped squirrel

Colobus monkey

Sedge-frog

Gorilla

Oleander hawkmoth

Banded duiker

These animals are found in the lower parts of an African rainforest. Some of them look for food on the forest floor, but return to the trees to sleep at night.

In the shade

The forest floor is the darkest, warmest part of the rainforest. The air is still and damp. Only plants that like the shade can live here. Many, like the bromeliad, have specially shaped leaves which can take in water from the air. There is no grass in the rainforest. The floor is covered with fallen leaves and twigs. Other plants, like mosses, and insects, like ants, also live on the forest floor.

The rainforest is a web of life. The picture shows the branch of a rainforest tree. It is covered with different plants. Many insects, like grasshoppers and centipedes, live among the plants.

Notodontid moth

Bromeliad

Noctuid moth

Ants

Orange orchid Maxilleria

Lichen

Ant-spider

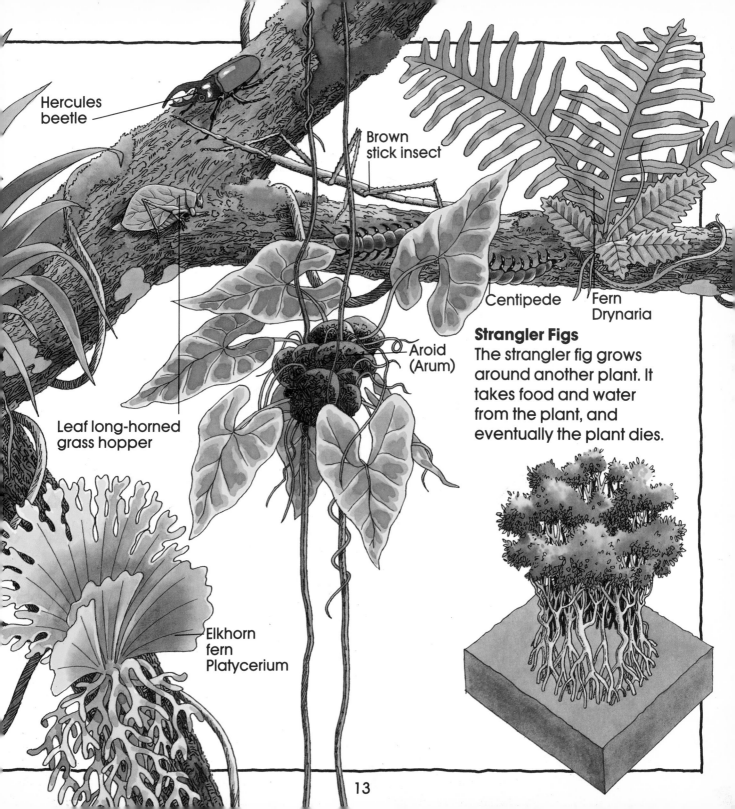

Hercules beetle

Brown stick insect

Centipede

Fern Drynaria

Strangler Figs
The strangler fig grows around another plant. It takes food and water from the plant, and eventually the plant dies.

Aroid (Arum)

Leaf long-horned grass hopper

Elkhorn fern Platycerium

13

The causes

Rainforest trees are cut down for lots of reasons. Many rainforest trees are very old – some over 200 years – and their wood is very hard. Hardwood is used for building houses and for making furniture. Yet it would be better to use cheaper woods like pine because pine can be grown in many countries in only 25 years, and new seedlings are planted when the trees are cut down. Large areas of rainforest are also cleared for animals to graze on.

The forest in the picture is being cut down, but it will not grow again. All the food for the forest plants comes from the trees, not the soil. When the trees are cut down, this food is lost. There is nothing left to grow crops with.

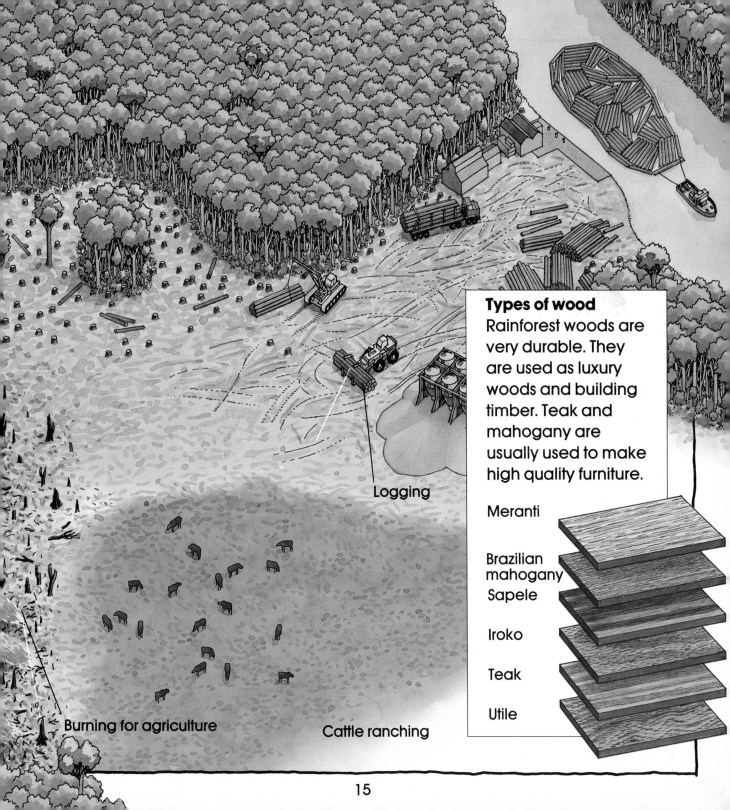

Logging

Types of wood
Rainforest woods are very durable. They are used as luxury woods and building timber. Teak and mahogany are usually used to make high quality furniture.

Meranti

Brazilian mahogany

Sapele

Iroko

Teak

Utile

Burning for agriculture

Cattle ranching

In danger

Plants and animals get used to the food and temperature in one place. If their homes are taken away, it is very difficult for them to survive in a different place. When we destroy a forest, the plants and animals living there are destroyed, too. All over the world many different kinds of plants and animals are disappearing because the trees are being cut down. Many of them are dying, or becoming extinct, which means they are gone forever.

Monkey-eating eagle
Philippines

Dove Langur
South Asia

Tiger
South Asia

Manatee
Amazon

Orangutan
South Asia

Aye aye
Madagascar

Jentink's duiker
West Africa

Indri
Madagascar

Gorilla
Africa

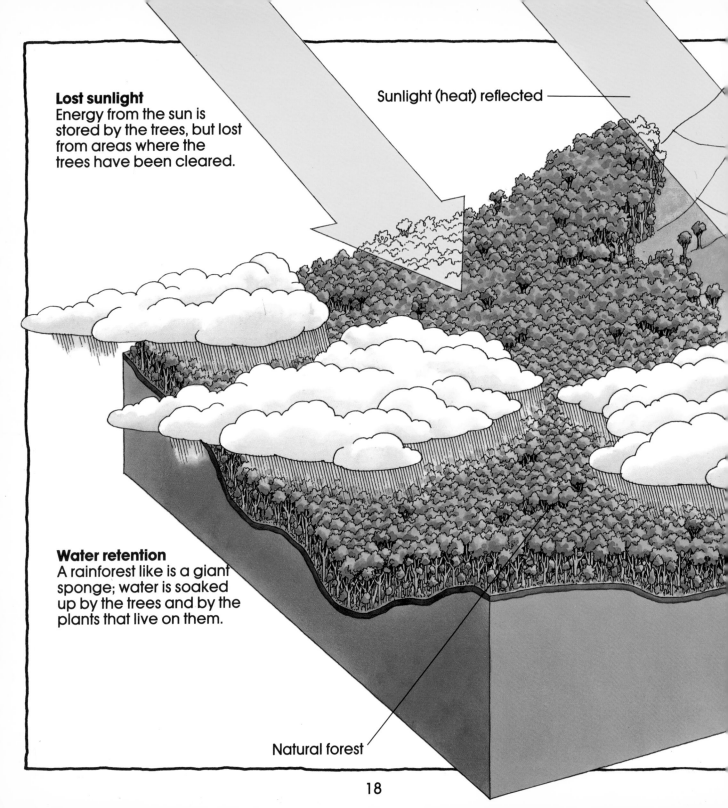

Lost sunlight
Energy from the sun is stored by the trees, but lost from areas where the trees have been cleared.

Sunlight (heat) reflected

Water retention
A rainforest like is a giant sponge; water is soaked up by the trees and by the plants that live on them.

Natural forest

The effects

Nothing is wasted in the rainforest. When it rains, the roots of the trees take in water. This water travels up the tree and into the leaves, where it is slowly released into the air. When the leaves fall they give the soil food. Cutting down the forests can be catastrophic. With the trees gone plants and animals lose their home, and there is nothing to hold the soil and water in place, which can cause floods.

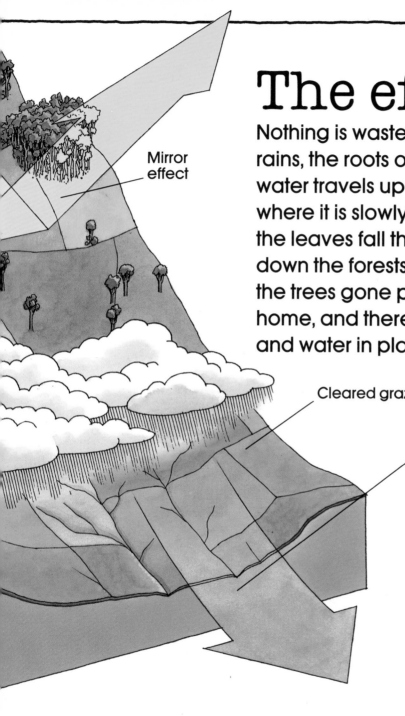

Mirror effect

Cleared grazing land

Soil erosion

The rainforest plays an important part in controlling the amount of water in the air. Clouds form above the forest from moisture given off by the leaves. The rain that falls is then reabsorbed by the trees. But if a forest is cleared water runs away.

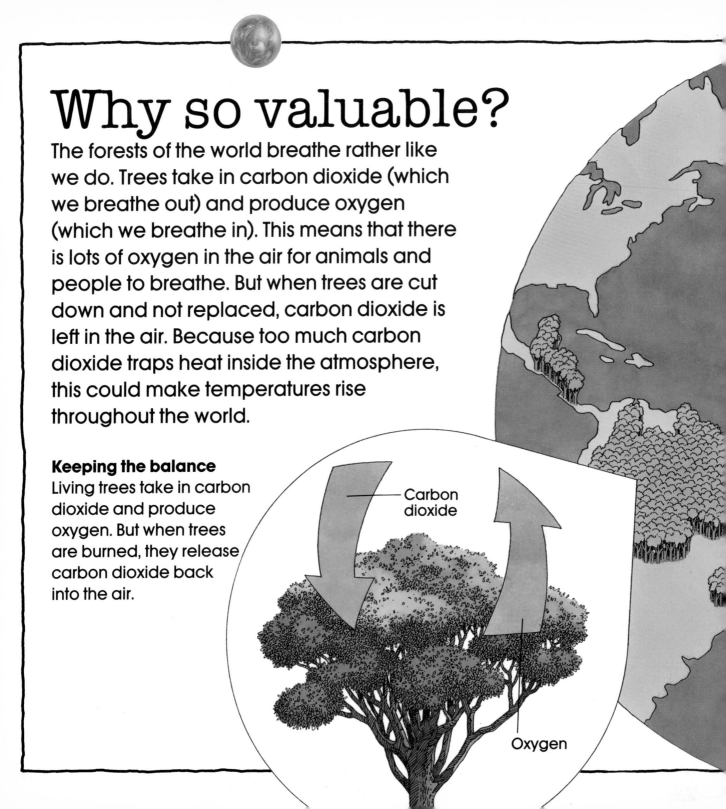

Why so valuable?

The forests of the world breathe rather like we do. Trees take in carbon dioxide (which we breathe out) and produce oxygen (which we breathe in). This means that there is lots of oxygen in the air for animals and people to breathe. But when trees are cut down and not replaced, carbon dioxide is left in the air. Because too much carbon dioxide traps heat inside the atmosphere, this could make temperatures rise throughout the world.

Keeping the balance
Living trees take in carbon dioxide and produce oxygen. But when trees are burned, they release carbon dioxide back into the air.

Carbon dioxide

Oxygen

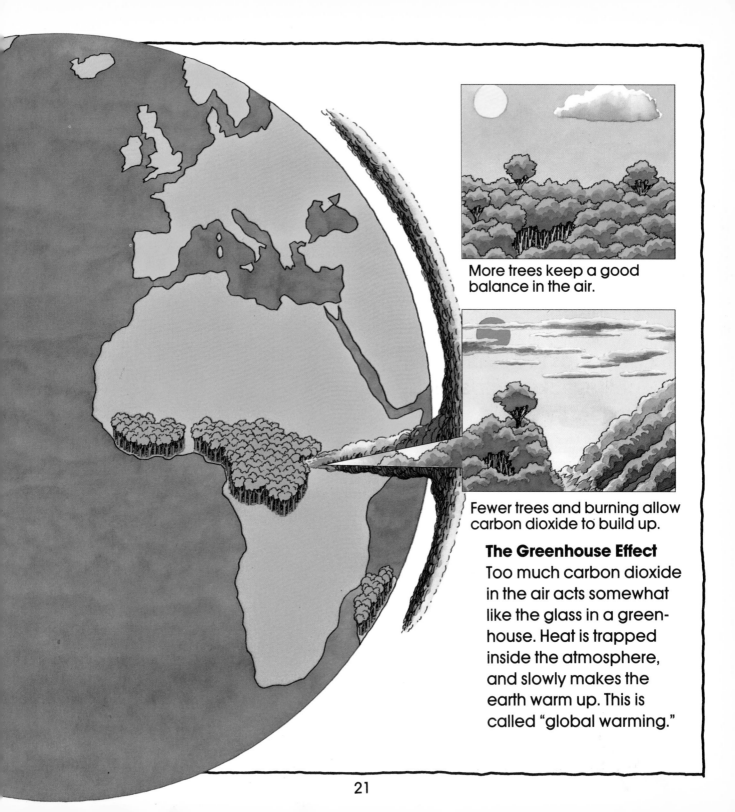

More trees keep a good balance in the air.

Fewer trees and burning allow carbon dioxide to build up.

The Greenhouse Effect

Too much carbon dioxide in the air acts somewhat like the glass in a green-house. Heat is trapped inside the atmosphere, and slowly makes the earth warm up. This is called "global warming."

Forest people

The people of the rainforest take everything they need from the forest, but do not harm it. They clear small areas for their crops and then move to a new place. The forest quickly grows again. The forest people also gather natural medicines from forest plants. They have a lot to teach us. But if we destroy their forest, they will start to disappear. Then we will not be able to learn from them.

Slash and burn
When the forest people cut down and burn a small patch of forest, the ash makes the soil richer. But only a small amount of food can be grown before the soil loses this richness. If this is done too often, the soil loses all its goodness and cannot be used for growing crops on.

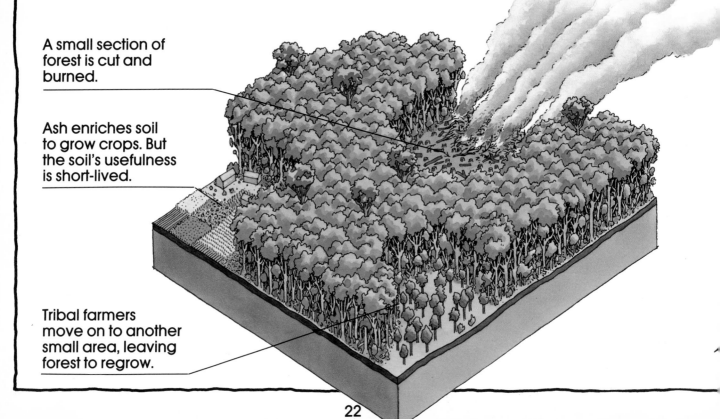

A small section of forest is cut and burned.

Ash enriches soil to grow crops. But the soil's usefulness is short-lived.

Tribal farmers move on to another small area, leaving forest to regrow.

Yam

Okra pods

Sweet peppers

Chilies

Cassava

Hunter gatherers
The forest people know the value and importance of everything in the forest. They hunt animals and collect berries, roots and fruits for food. They also know which plants can heal wounds, cure stomachaches and make sick people well.

Forest riches

Many of the things that we use every day come from the rainforest. Bananas, coffee, tea and spices like cinnamon were first found growing naturally in the rainforest. Some perfumes are made from rainforest plants. Many of the plants that grow there are important because they give us medicines. Nobody knows how many other useful materials have not yet been found.

Saving lives

The forest people use lots of different plants as medicines. The Madagascar rosy periwinkle (shown below) can be used to fight serious illnesses.

What can we find?
No one knows how many useful plants there may still be in the rainforest. But, unless they are protected, they may be destroyed before they are discovered.

Rosy periwinkle

Pineapple and exotic fruits

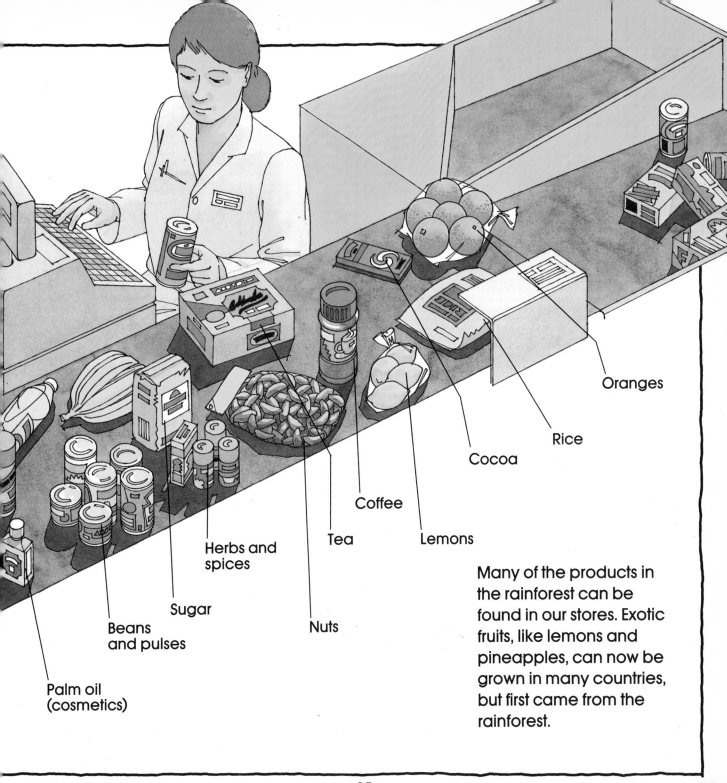

Oranges

Rice

Cocoa

Coffee

Lemons

Tea

Herbs and spices

Nuts

Sugar

Beans and pulses

Palm oil (cosmetics)

Many of the products in the rainforest can be found in our stores. Exotic fruits, like lemons and pineapples, can now be grown in many countries, but first came from the rainforest.

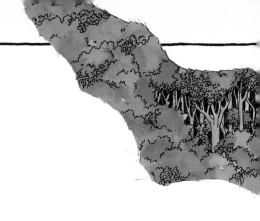

People power

If the rainforests disappear, many valuable materials also disappear. The homes of thousands of plants, animals and people are lost. It is therefore vital that people start working together to save the rainforests, by protecting what remains and by planting new trees. Governments must teach people about the importance of the rainforests and the things that grow there.

Caring about trees
Famous rock stars, like Sting, have organized events to raise money. This money is used for projects to save the rainforest and its people.

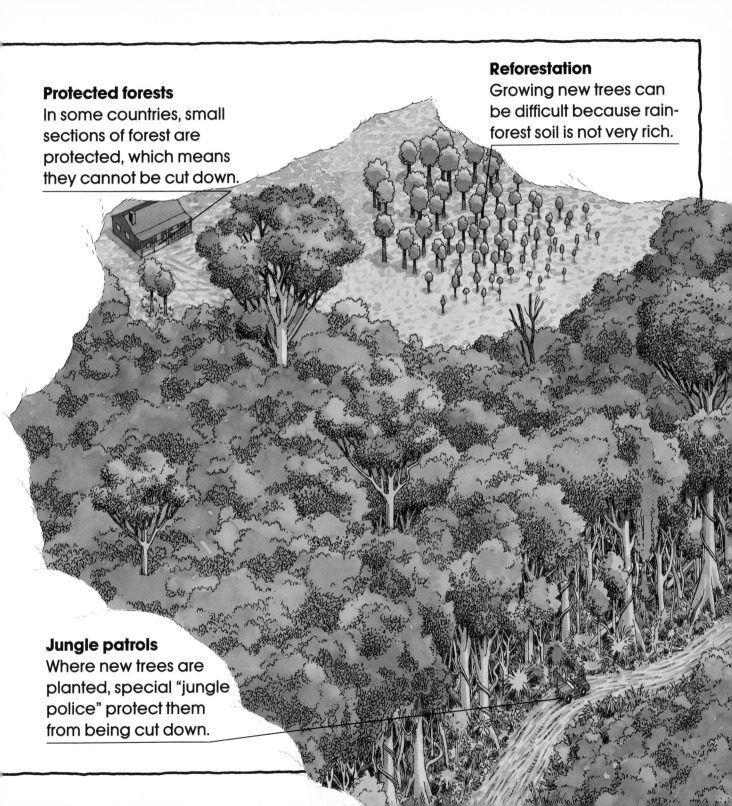

Protected forests
In some countries, small sections of forest are protected, which means they cannot be cut down.

Reforestation
Growing new trees can be difficult because rainforest soil is not very rich.

Jungle patrols
Where new trees are planted, special "jungle police" protect them from being cut down.

Forest file

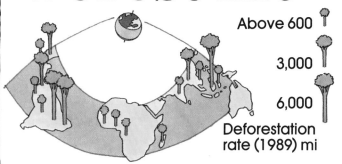

Above 600

3,000

6,000

Deforestation rate (1989) mi

Disappearing forests

Twenty years ago forests, including tropical rainforests, covered about one-quarter of the land in the world. Today they cover a much smaller area. In a few years' time, there will only be very small forests left.

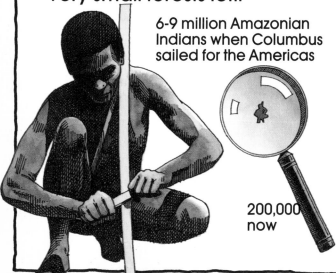

6-9 million Amazonian Indians when Columbus sailed for the Americas

200,000 now

People in danger

Rainforest people have nearly lost their homes and their lives twice. Explorers with guns came first. Then more people came and cut down the forest.

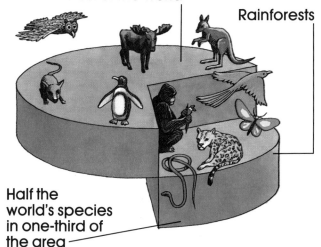

Rest of the world

Rainforests

Half the world's species in one-third of the area

Brimming with life

Rainforests that have not been disturbed are full of wildlife. In a small piece of rainforest there are over 1,500 kinds of flowering plants, 750 kinds of trees, 125 kinds of mammals, 400 kinds of birds, 150 different butterflies and many other insects.

Forest flooding

Large areas of rainforest land have been cleared and flooded with water to make dams. This means that they cannot be used to grow trees or food on ever again.

Poisoned arrows

The poison from the yellow tree frog is used by Amazonian Indians when they hunt. It makes an animal's muscles stop working. This poison can now be used to relax people's muscles before an operation.

Blocking the waterways

When rainforest trees and plants are taken away, mud washes off the land and can block up nearby rivers and canals.

Some of the largest and smallest animals in the world live in the African rainforest. Giants include the goliath frog (5), African land snail (2), and goliath beetle (3). The longest insect is the Indonesian giant stick insect (4), the largest butterfly is the Queen Alexandria birdwing (7) and the longest spider is the bird-eating spider (8). The huge elephant shrew (6) is nearly as big as the tiny royal antelope.

Adult African pygmies measure only 5 ft (1.5m).

Glossary

Atmosphere
The layer of gases that surrounds and protects the earth. It is about 450mi deep.

Bacteria
Tiny organisms with only one cell. They were the earliest forms of life on earth over 300 million years ago. Bacteria cause decay and diseases, and spoil food.

Equator
An imaginary line drawn around the middle of the earth. It is an equal distance from the north and south poles.

Extinct
When every member of a type of animal or plant dies, the species is said to be extinct. This means that it is gone for ever.

Greenhouse Effect
The normal process by which heat is kept in the lower atmosphere. Without it life could not live on earth. But if too much heat is trapped, temperatures could go up, and this would be dangerous to life.

Hardwood
The tough timber from broad-leaved, deciduous trees.

Tropics
The hottest part of the earth. The tropics are a strip which crosses the Equator.

Understory
The lower canopy level in a rainforest. Young plants of the upper canopy grow here, as do fruits like the banana.

Index